Nights With The Moon

4:44 AM

Kristen Saia

BookLeaf Publishing
India | USA | UK

Made with ❤ on the BookLeaf Publishing Platform
www.bookleafpub.in
www.bookleafpub.com

Dedication

For the women who loved too hard,
who forgave too much,
who stayed longer than they should have,
and still found the courage to leave.

For the hearts that broke but kept beating,
for the hands that learned to hold themselves,
for the voices that shook but never went silent.

For the version of me that thought the pain would never end,
and for the version of you, reading this now,
searching for a way back to yourself.

To the one who left:
thank you for the lesson,
but this story was never yours to finish.

And to you, dear reader:
Go. Take back your light.

Preface

Before you begin, I want you to know this:
I did not write these words with a steady hand.
I wrote them between sobs, in the hollow quiet of nights that stretched too long.
I wrote them while my heart was still learning how to beat on its own again.
I wrote them when I did not believe I would survive the weight of my own breaking.
But I did.
And you will, too.
This book is not a love story.
This is a resurrection.
This is a fire that burned everything I thought I was, and this is what I built from the ashes.

Acknowledgements

To the lessons disguised as lovers — thank you for teaching me who I never want to be.

One

You didn't break me—
not all the way.
just enough
to make me quieter,
more careful
with where I placed my joy.

You loved like a guest
who never unpacked.
always ready to go,
even when you said you'd stay.

I wrote your name
in the steam on my bathroom mirror.
watched it disappear,
just like you did.

And still,
I stayed soft.
still held the door open

for love,
even after it walked out
without saying goodbye.

This heart—
it bruises easy
but it beats loud.
And someday
someone will hear it
and stay
just long enough
to call it home.

Two

He came with jokes
and soft eyes,
knew how to make me laugh
when I was mid-cry,
like he'd done it before—
like he made a habit
of saving women
he couldn't stay for.

He made blueberry pie
like it was nothing.
Said love was in the crust,
but never stuck around
long enough to prove it.

We didn't fight.
we didn't fall apart.
he just vanished—
quiet as a sigh,
loud as a door that never closed.

Some people leave
like they forgot something.
He left like he remembered
something better.

I still think about that pie sometimes.
how it tasted like August,
how he kissed me with sugar
on his lips,
and a goodbye
already in his throat.

Three

There's a sadness
I can't shake,
like the tide
that never leaves,
only pulls harder
the closer it gets.

The moon looks down,
unmoved,
cold in its beauty—
it pulls at the water,
but doesn't care
if it drowns.

I watch it,
and I feel the weight—
that this pain
isn't a visitor,
it's a resident.

It comes,
it goes,
but it always returns,
tearing at the shore,
like love
that never knew how to let go.

And I wonder—
is it supposed to be this way?
endless,
merciless,
a quiet ache
that keeps coming back
like the tide,
whether I'm ready or not.

Four

I slept on your side
for a week
just to prove
you weren't coming back.

The bed kept its silence
like a witness unwilling to lie.
Sheets pressed into the shape of absence,
pillows folded themselves around emptiness,
and the mattress hummed
with the gravity of a body no longer there.

Every morning, the empty bed
was a cathedral of loss.
I measured its vastness with my ribs,
traced the gaps where your weight should have been,
and found only the echo
of a presence that refused to return.

I slept there anyway,

a trespasser in a space
that had already been claimed
by memory, silence, and absence.

Five

It wasn't slow,
wasn't soft—
he didn't ease out
like most people do.
He just got up,
said I'm leaving you,
and turned away.

No fight,
no last kiss,
no we should've tried harder.
Just him,
walking out
like it was nothing.

I stood there,
frozen,
fighting the weight of his absence
before he was even gone.

I wanted to scream,
wanted to throw things,
wanted to make him feel the hole
he was leaving in me.
but the silence said it all.

He didn't want to fight.
didn't even want to say goodbye.
Just wanted to walk out
like he hadn't spent years
turning my world into his.

I don't know what's worse—
the way he left
or the way I still look for him
in the spaces he used to fill.

Six

Peace, I think,
arrives without ceremony.

It settles where expectation
finally loosens its grip,
where the question mark
softens into a pause.

I stopped reaching
for the other side of the sheets,
not because I forgot you,
but because my hands
grew tired of asking.

This is not giving up.

It is giving in
to the truth that some loves
are meant to pass through us—
not stay.

And still,
the bed holds me.
The night does not collapse.
I remain.

Seven

There's something in the way
the sun rises now—
gentle,
like it understands
the weight of everything I've carried.

I no longer reach for you
in the dark,
but I still feel
the hollow places
where you used to fit.

Healing isn't loud.
it doesn't scream
or beg for attention.
It's a quiet thing,
like water carving a path
through stone—
slow,
but undeniable.

Each day,
I take a little less
of you with me.
and though I'll never be
who I was,
I'm learning
to be something new
without you.

Eight

I don't talk about you much anymore.
There are places in me
that remember your hands
even though I don't reach for them now.

Healing came quiet—
not all at once,
but in small ways.

Making coffee
without thinking of you.
laughing
without guilt.
Looking in the mirror
and seeing
only me.

You left,
but I stayed.
and that,

I've learned,

was always enough.

Nine

What they meant to break
turned to gold in your hands.

This is the secret:
you were always the fire.

Ten

You've been chipped,
you've been cracked,
but you are not broken.

The earth itself
is a collection of fractures—
and still,
it holds the weight of mountains.

What you call broken
is only the process
of becoming something
stronger
than what you were.

Eleven

I found your lies folded neat in the laundry.
I held them like old shirts, pressed them to my chest,
wondering if I missed the stain or
if I wanted to pretend it wasn't there.

You left so quietly,
like you were never here at all.
Like I imagined your mouth on my mouth.
Your promises –
cheap glass dressed as crystal.

She wears your smile now.
I hope it fits her better than it fit me.
It always felt too sharp around the edges.

You are happy.
I watch it unfold in pictures I no longer save,
but still look at
when the house feels too quiet
and my body remembers the shape of your absence.

I do not want you back.
I want back the girl who believed you.
The girl who slept with both eyes closed.
The girl who kissed you
like the world wasn't ending.

I bury her carefully.
Water her grief.
Sing to her at night.

One day, she will bloom
into someone you will not recognize.
Someone I will not apologize for.

Twelve

I wanted revenge,
until I wanted freedom.
I wanted to scorch you from my memory,
burn every photograph into ash.

Dreamed of you watching me thrive
with hunger in your eyes,
your mouth full of regret,
choking on my name.

But vengeance is a leash,
and I was never meant to be tethered.
So I dropped the match,
let the fire consume only what needed to die —
the ache, the asking, the endless if-onlys.

I unhooked you from my ribs,
pulled out your ghost like an old nail,
and for the first time,
my breath did not taste like smoke.

I do not wait for you to see me healed.
I do not wait for you at all.

Thirteen

To the girl I used to be:
I am sorry I doubted you.
I am sorry I made you beg for love
from hands too careless to hold you right.

You were always enough.
You were always gold beneath the rust,
a lighthouse waiting for her own storm to pass.

If I could reach back through time,
I would pull you close,
brush the salt from your cheeks,
whisper in your ear:
you survive this.
you survive him.
you survive yourself.

Look at us now –
rooted, radiant, untamed.
No longer asking to be chosen.

No longer folding ourselves small enough to fit in someone else's story.

We are the story.
We are the fire and the bloom.
We are the proof:
even from ruin,
life can begin again.

Fourteen

The room stayed quiet.

Nothing rushed in to save me.
So I learned the weight of my own palms,
how steadiness can exist
without witness.

I held my own hands—
not as comfort,
but as proof.

For the first time,
I didn't brace for impact.
I didn't shrink
at the sound of my own breathing.

That was the day I chose myself.
Not triumphantly.
Not loudly.

Just finally.

Fifteen

Years from now
I'll remember this version of me
like the city I once mistook
for the whole map—
too loud,
too convincing.

I won't remember what I was waiting for.

Only how sure I was
that everything important
was happening there.

It wasn't.

I won't be healed.
I won't be wiser.
I'll just be elsewhere—
crossing a street,
missing a train,

buying fruit I don't need.

The light will change.
Traffic will move.
Someone will laugh behind me.

I step forward
with everyone else.

Sixteen

You left for a job—
but it wasn't the job.

It was someone else
who fit your next act.

I was a scene,
timed and disposable,
cut when the laugh ran thin.

The house lights are up.
The audience is gone.

A role never written for me
was never mine to play.

No applause required.
No audience waiting.

Just the rhythm of breath,

the weight of a hand on a doorknob.
The quiet thrill of doors opening
I had never noticed before.

Seventeen

Little one,
you didn't imagine it—
you were handed a life
with more weight than most.

You learned early
how to carry things alone,
how to choose the steep path
even when no one asked you to climb.

You thought pain was proof.
That endurance meant worth.
That love had to hurt
to be real.

I know.

I walked that way for years.
But listen—
you didn't choose the hard road

because you were broken.

You chose it
because you were strong
before you knew you could rest.

You made it through
what should have stopped you.
You kept your softness
when it would've been easier
to sharpen.

One day you'll learn
that survival isn't the same as punishment.
That ease isn't a betrayal.
That joy doesn't have to be earned
through suffering.

And when you finally stop bracing,
the world won't collapse.

It will open.

You don't have to prove anything anymore.
You already made it.

Eighteen

Strength is not always loud.

It is the quiet pulse of stars
dancing in the velvet of night,
the gentle sway of tides
that carry worlds without notice.

It is the wind weaving through trees,
the sunlight tracing edges of clouds,
the small gravity in your chest
that keeps your feet on the ground
while your heart reaches skyward.

Even in stillness,
it moves and nudges time forward.

Even in shadows, it shines.

Even alone, it is yours—
and the universe leans,

just slightly,
to follow.

Nineteen

The past has no hold here,
it is a whisper in the wind,
a story told by those who don't know
the weight of a woman's rise.

She has walked through fire,
and left it all behind,
her feet lighter than air,
her heart unburdened by regret.

She does not seek permission to be,
to bloom,
to claim the earth beneath her.

The world is hers,
wide and open.
A canvas waiting for her touch.

There is no fear in her step,
no hesitation in her eyes.

She moves with the grace
of a bird in flight,
no longer bound by the expectations of yesterday.

Twenty

You will feel broken.
You will feel small.

You will remember the spaces
they left behind.
And that is okay.

Because even in the cracks,
even in the quiet,
you are gathering yourself,
collecting the pieces
that were always yours to hold.

The heart lets go
so what is meant for you
can find its way in.

The spaces they left
are not empty—they are waiting,
ready to be filled

with light you have yet to know.

The days will come
when the streets hum under your feet,
wind brushes your hair,
sunlight traces your shoulders,
and your own heartbeat
feels like home.

You will carry your own warmth.
You will carry your own voice.

And one day,
the memory of what left you
will be a window,
not a wall.
A place to see the sky
opening for what is truly yours.

Keep going, I am with you.

"The strongest women are the ones who have known defeat, known suffering, known struggle, and have found their way out of the depths." — K. L. Toth

www.ingramcontent.com/pod-product-compliance
Lightning Source LLC
Chambersburg PA
CBHW051742130826
49812CB00033B/967
9789370926066